WHAT JESUS IS LIKE

What Jesus Is Like

Concepción Cabrera de Armida

Translated by
Most Reverend Donald W. Montrose
Former Bishop of Stockton, California

ST PAULS

Library of Congress Cataloging-in-Publication Data

Conchita. 1862-1937.
  [Cómo es Jesús. English]
  What Jesus is like / Concepción Cabrera de Armida; translated by
Most Reverend Donald W. Montrose.
        p. cm.
    ISBN 978-0-8189-1266-5
    1. Jesus Christ—Person and offices.   I. Title.

    BT203.C6613   2008
    232—dc22

                                                    2008001275

Produced and designed in the United States of America by the
Fathers and Brothers of the Society of St. Paul,
2187 Victory Boulevard, Staten Island, New York 10314-6603
as part of their communications apostolate.

ISBN-10: 0-8189-1266-9
ISBN-13: 978-0-8189-1266-5

Printing Information:

Current Printing - first digit   1   2   3   4   5   6   7   8   9   10

Year of Current Printing - first year shown

2008 2009 2010 2011 2012 2013 2014 2015 2016 2017

ACKNOWLEDGMENTS

Sr. Dolores Icaza Conrey, R.C.S.C.J.
Davina Werthmann
James Wierzbicki
Ron Leonardo
Louise Alberti

TABLE OF CONTENTS

INTRODUCTION

The publication of *What Jesus Is Like* written by the Venerable Concepción Cabrera de Armida, is very timely and providential in order that we might fall in love with Jesus, Our Lord, Redeemer and Savior, God and Man. He Whom all Christians wish to reproduce in themselves through love, as Conchita herself says in the edition which she personally promoted.

The objective which we see characterizing this age is twofold: (1) "the proclamation of Jesus Christ as our life and our hope," and (2) "the commitment of ourselves to work in the spirit of the new evangelization and of the new millennium toward a more evangelical and more missionary Church, a more just and unified society and a culture of life and hope."

We believe that if we want to form a culture open to moral values, it is necessary to continue insisting that the laity assume their rightful place, especially in education and in the means of communication.

Narco-trafficking, sects, and the materialistic environment that smothers us are problems that can only be illuminated by Jesus Christ, the son of Mary, Redeemer of all. That is why this edition of *What Jesus Is Like* is providential and very timely. It will be like a breath of fresh air in the midst of so much ideological corruption that scatters us and in the midst of so much noise that debilitates us. Only Jesus is light, only He is the Living Water, the Way, the Truth and the Life. He is our hope.

I express here my lively congratulations to those who have supervised the edition of this precious book. I also admire and congratulate those who are going to meditate upon it, especially the young people, who are hungering for life models; surely they shall know how to enjoy it in depth. Only He has words of eternal life, as Simon Peter said when it seemed that everyone had abandoned Jesus in the face of the news of His presence in the Eucharist (cf. Gospel of St. John, 6).

May the Virgin Mary, Our Mother of Guadalupe, continue to be for us the teacher who teaches us *What Jesus Is Like*.

México, D.F.
December 12, 1997, Year of Jesus Christ
102nd Anniversary of the Pontifical Coronation
of Our Lady of Guadalupe

> ✠ Ramón Godínez Flores
> Auxiliary Bishop of Guadalajara
> Secretary General of the
> Mexican Episcopal Conference

PROLOGUE

The sole purpose of these pages is to cause us to fall in love with Jesus, our Savior and Redeemer, true God and true man. He is the One Whom all of us Christians should wish to imitate in our lives by our love.

Concepción Cabrera de Armida

BIBLICAL ABBREVIATIONS

OLD TESTAMENT

Genesis	Gn	Nehemiah	Ne	Baruch	Ba
Exodus	Ex	Tobit	Tb	Ezekiel	Ezk
Leviticus	Lv	Judith	Jdt	Daniel	Dn
Numbers	Nb	Esther	Est	Hosea	Ho
Deuteronomy	Dt	1 Maccabees	1 M	Joel	Jl
Joshua	Jos	2 Maccabees	2 M	Amos	Am
Judges	Jg	Job	Jb	Obadiah	Ob
Ruth	Rt	Psalms	Ps	Jonah	Jon
1 Samuel	1 S	Proverbs	Pr	Micah	Mi
2 Samuel	2 S	Ecclesiastes	Ec	Nahum	Na
1 Kings	1 K	Song of Songs	Sg	Habakkuk	Hab
2 Kings	2 K	Wisdom	Ws	Zephaniah	Zp
1 Chronicles	1 Ch	Sirach	Si	Haggai	Hg
2 Chronicles	2 Ch	Isaiah	Is	Malachi	Ml
Ezra	Ezr	Jeremiah	Jr	Zechariah	Zc
		Lamentations	Lm		

NEW TESTAMENT

Matthew	Mt	Ephesians	Eph	Hebrews	Heb
Mark	Mk	Philippians	Ph	James	Jm
Luke	Lk	Colossians	Col	1 Peter	1 P
John	Jn	1 Thessalonians	1 Th	2 Peter	2 P
Acts	Ac	2 Thessalonians	2 Th	1 John	1 Jn
Romans	Rm	1 Timothy	1 Tm	2 John	2 Jn
1 Corinthians	1 Cor	2 Timothy	2 Tm	3 John	3 Jn
2 Corinthians	2 Cor	Titus	Tt	Jude	Jude
Galatians	Gal	Philemon	Phm	Revelation	Rv

DEDICATION

My Jesus, I dedicate these pages to You, wishing that they were of fire in order to inflame hearts that they might fall in love with You, the God-Man, with You, Who are both human and divine.

I want to contribute a bit so that You will become better known. So that in contemplating *What Jesus Is Like* they might fall in love with You.

When our faith does not illuminate our hearts, in vain does human reason struggle to comprehend. However, You are the Light of the world that illuminates all things. You are the Font of Living Water that satiates our thirst for the sacred. You are everything to us, my Jesus. Grant that our world might know You more and more, so that it may be converted into a conflagration of holy love.

Through Mary's immaculate hands, I present to You these pages written from my heart. May she, who knew better than anyone else on earth what Jesus is really like, print You upon our understanding and pluck from us a loving resonance of gratitude toward You, that will resound even to heaven and will console Your Divine Heart.

WHAT JESUS IS LIKE

1

HIS PHYSICAL APPEARANCE

What supernatural beauty must Jesus' physical appearance have had!

Jesus is not known. That is why He is not loved! How handsome Jesus was and is! What beauty, what clarity, what transparency, what an infinite depth of all perfection!

There is not a single ray of light that does not emanate from that Sun, nor a single divine ardor that does not come from that central point, nor a single drop of heavenly joy that is not derived from that Font.

Knowing Him, studying Him and feeling His presence, who would be capable of offending Him? One must manifest Him, taste Him, penetrate Him, but more than anything, one must *love* Him, because love draws us closer to Him. Love is a light that illuminates, transforms and unites.

To be united to Jesus is to have surrendered to the will of the Father.

To be united with Jesus is to be one with Him in thought and affections. It is to imitate, in the poverty of our souls, the habitual and intimate state of Jesus' soul, a reflection, in its own right, of the interior depths of the Divine Word.

Prayer

O Mary, who in this world has known the beauty of Jesus as you have? Show Him to me. Give Him to me. For He is also mine. Cause me to imitate Him, to love Him, to sacrifice myself for His sake, in order to give you many souls who might glorify Him here on earth and eternally at your side later.

May these meditations on *What Jesus Is Like*, written in the warmth of your maternal heart, serve to let Him be known better both in His love and in His sorrow. I would consider myself blessed if I were able to procure from each reader a single act of fervent love to offer it to Him as a remembrance of my journey upon this earth.

2

HIS DIVINITY

*"The Word became flesh and made His
dwelling among us" (Jn 1:14).*

Jesus was not only a man; He was the God-
Man.

Let us think about Jesus a great deal and
often, seeing Him as not just the human person
that He was, but also as the God-Man. Seeing
God in the human person, seeing divinity united
to humanity, becoming translucent in this most
Holy Humanity.

If Jesus is handsome, it is because He
reflects divine beauty. If Jesus is divinely good,
compassionate, loving and tender; if He is sensitive, attractive, most pure and most holy, it
is because of His divinity, which is one and the
same in the Father and the Holy Spirit.

One must see and experience Jesus such
as He is — divine and human — so that we
can better comprehend and be more grate-

ful for the humiliation of the Incarnate Word upon becoming man in Mary's virginal womb without ever ceasing to be God, being moved only by love, by His infinite generosity toward us sinners.

In that divinity which we can scarcely glimpse, the Father Who is Light is present, the Son, Who is Light from Light, is present, and the Holy Spirit, Eternal Center of Eternal Light, is present. Let us not close the eyes of our soul to this uncreated Light, to divinity itself, even if it should blind us, should annihilate us. For thus we shall comprehend something of our nothingness and at the same time we shall rejoice in Him Who is everything.

It is very sad, but very common, to treat Jesus as if He were merely a man, without recognizing the Divine Word within Him, without meditating on or even thinking about the fact that He is the God-Man, that divinity is present within Him.

The Most Holy Humanity of Jesus is like a door, or a path, or a stepping-stone. For us to approach divinity, one must pass through that Most Sacred Humanity to reach it. The divinity of Jesus is life itself. It is the Light of the World. It is the Eternal Truth without shadow.

Prayer

O Lord, You are my repose, my happiness, my thanksgiving, my portion and my only love. I have no virtues, but You possess them all, and You are mine, divine and human. Having You, I have all I need to pay my debts and to make amends to the Divinity offended by my sins, that I may be purified and enter into heaven.

O Mary, obtain for us from God that Light that will eclipse the things of earth, that Clarity that transcends the visible, so that we may be able to enter into the sanctuary of the Heart of Jesus. We want to be able to take abode in that God-Man. We want to lose ourselves in the unfathomable depths of His love and rejoice even here in this earthly exile, knowing through you what Jesus is like. That He is all love, and is ever seeking our love. Amen.

3

HIS LOVE FOR HIS FATHER

*"Through the eternal Spirit [Christ] offered Himself
unblemished to God" (Heb 9:14).*

The only One Who understands Christ is the
Father. *"No one knows who the Son is except the Father"* (Lk 10:22). In order to understand Jesus,
insofar as that is possible, one must perceive
Him as a reflection of the Father.

In Jesus the God-Man, the Father sees all
of creation. In His Word (the Son) — Who is a
mirror in which He sees Himself — the Father
is reflected and is unified. The Father contem-
plates all of humanity united to Christ's Body,
with Jesus as head of that Body. The Father,
with His Divine Glance, looks not only for the
creature, but also for Jesus in the creature. He
sees Himself in Jesus and in the creature.

Jesus, under the guidance of the Holy
Spirit, ordered everything in His mortal life

according to the will of His Father. That is why the final consummation of the mysteries of Jesus was His ascension to the Father. He offered Himself through the Holy Spirit in the midst of His intense suffering to His heavenly Father.

The love of Jesus for His Father is a priestly love: that is, a love which glorifies, a love which immolates itself, a love which redeems and saves; a love which reached its climactic fulfillment on Calvary and which perpetuates itself in the Mass and in souls. It is as though Jesus wished to fill heaven and earth, time and eternity with His love for the Father. The love of Jesus for His Father first overflowed in Him and then was poured out over His entire Mystical Body. Our poor love is nothing more than the effect of that Divine Love of Jesus for His Father.

Following Jesus' example, we will love the Father, on behalf of all those souls who do not love Him. We will make every effort so that the Father will not miss even a spark of that love. We will love Him in union with Jesus. With a love that glorifies Him. A love that immolates itself. A love that redeems and saves! We will love Him with a love which finds, like the love of Jesus did, its crowning glory in the cross, in Christ's sacrifice, which we should offer at every moment unceasingly to the Father, one with that Divine Redeemer.

Prayer

O heavenly Father, our love is in reality so very small and imperfect, so deficient and inconstant. But Jesus has loved You for us. The poor love that our hearts now offer You comes from the Heart of Your Son. Do You not recognize its fragrance, the unique perfume of Jesus?

We love You, O heavenly Father, with all our heart, with all our soul and with all our strength. We cry out to You with the holy enthusiasm and abandonment to Your Will which Jesus did, for that Will was His food and His drink.

4

HIS LOVE FOR THE HOLY SPIRIT

"The Holy Spirit will come upon you,
and the power of the Most High will overshadow
you. Therefore the child to be born will be called
holy, the Son of God" (Lk 1:35).

The Holy Spirit was the very life of Jesus. And Jesus did not act except under His divine influence. How grateful Jesus was for the flawlessness and splendor with which the Spirit adorned His Soul with all the virtues from the very first moment of His Incarnation. The effort, shall I say, with which He endowed the immaculate body of the Word become flesh and His most Sacred Heart with the most sublime and generous sentiments.

This divine Holy Spirit used His immense power and His infinite riches to form Jesus in Mary and to give us an ineffable model of all humanity in Him.

The Holy Spirit is united to Jesus from the moment of His Incarnation until His death. All Jesus' life was lived under His divine influence.

Later, Mary had scarcely begun to speak to her cousin Elizabeth, when she and St. John — who was to prepare the way for the Messiah — received the Holy Spirit.

At the time of the circumcision, the Holy Spirit descended upon the Blood of Jesus. And when Mary and Joseph took Jesus to the temple in Jerusalem, *"the Holy Spirit led Simeon, in fulfillment of His promise, that he might see Him"* (cf. Lk 2:25-32).

The Holy Spirit led Jesus into the desert: *"Filled with the Holy Spirit, Jesus returned from the Jordan and was led by the Spirit into the desert"* (Lk 4:1). Likewise, St. Augustine tells us that a new anointing with the Spirit was manifested to the world at the Jordan River when Jesus was baptized by John the Baptist. A voice came from the heavens saying, *"This is My beloved Son, in Whom I am well pleased"* (Mt 3:17). St. Luke clearly demonstrates that He was anointed when he writes: *"Jesus, full of the Holy Spirit, returned from the Jordan"* (cf. Lk 4:1).

During the final days of His life, Jesus, our Model and Teacher of all the virtues, spoke only about love. He asked for love from Him Who is Love Itself, from the Person Who is Love, and He promised the gift of the Spirit of Love. This Jesus, Who is God and man, gives us the Holy Spirit; as man, this is His prayer for us, and as the God that He is, He gives Him to us. Later, we will hear Him say to the apostles, *"Receive the Holy Spirit."* Of Christ it has been said, *"Christ will baptize them with the Holy Spirit and with fire"* (cf. Mt 3:11).

Prayer

O Mary, most faithful spouse of the Holy Spirit, with your most pure lips say thank you to Jesus on our behalf. Thank Him for the glory of the Father, of the Son, and of that most beloved Holy Spirit. Amen.

5

HIS NAME

"Because of this, God greatly exalted Him and bestowed on Him the name that is above every name" (Ph 2:9).

Jesus' Name is a Name of love, of suffering and of hope! But what a price Jesus paid to receive this most sweet Name which means Savior!

What a sweet Name is Jesus' Name! What a heavenly sentiment one feels when pronouncing it! How much the soul glimpses through this Name! There is something very pure, very beautiful and harmonious in it. Something made up of light and purity. Of love and suffering. Of fidelity and of loyalty! Something which one cannot look at full on, because it is blinding. Which one cannot embrace without caution, because it melts one. Which, nevertheless, in all Its Light the soul longs to contemplate and to embrace without any limits.

Jesus is a Name of peace which calms all storms. A Name of light which illuminates the nights of the spirit. A Name which embraces and consoles. Which sustains and gives one the strength for sacrifice. A Name which penetrates even to the inner recesses of hearts and purifies them. A Name of glory and splendor. A Name that tastes of heaven. Adorable Name! Who is not enchanted by Your sweetness? Who does not experience Your virtue?

At times I see Him as a child. The first thing you ask a child is, "What's your name?" Let us do this often with Jesus. He will answer in the depths of our soul. With the sweetness and love that are so characteristic of Him, He will tell us what we need to hear. *"I am the Resurrection and the Life"* (Jn 11:25). His Divine Lips will tell us over and over that our faith will be illuminated and our hope for future happiness will expand the breadth of our souls, anguished at the thought of the death of those we love.

"It is I. Do not be afraid" (Mk 6:50). We shall hear, be touched and feel ourselves relieved of a great weight that oppresses us as we become aware of His Compassion, His Charity, and His Infinite Love. Jesus wants love from us more than fear. He wants more confidence, abandonment, love and gratefulness. How can we fear Him Who came to earth to save us?

Jesus is mine! Is it possible? Jesus is mine? Jesus is truly mine? Mine, that God Whom we bear in our soul and Who has surrendered Himself to us in a thousand excesses of love? Very well, then, let us offer ourselves to be His, all His, ever His. With all the sincerity, all the ardor, and all the effusion of our affection. In that word "Yours" let us place our being and our life. Yours for whatever You might wish, my Jesus. Yours to immolate myself. Yours for life, for death and for all eternity.

Prayer

O Most Holy Virgin, why did you give Him to us if not that we should constantly try to love Him as you loved Him? Thank you, Mary, my Mother. We beg you to place in our hearts, on our lips and in our souls that precious imprint, that Divine Seal that is ever saying to us: "Jesus, Jesus, Jesus!" Amen.

6

HIS HEART

"Take My yoke upon you and learn from Me,
for I am gentle and humble of heart"
(Mt 11:29).

Everything about Jesus is to be admired. His words, His gazes, His smile, His thoughts and actions, but most of all His incomparable Heart, Center and Fount of those allurements! In Him are encompassed all virtues and perfections: His holiness and His love. His Infinite, Ardent, Pure and Divine Love.

Nothing is more demanding and yet more tender and precious than that Heart in which every holy affection could be seen to radiate.

But that which is most admirable in the Heart of Jesus is His serenity in His intimate sufferings, in that interior cross which tortured His soul from the instant of the Incarnation until His death. In His most Sacred Heart, Jesus felt the piercing thorns of all our suffering and the bitterness of all our tears.

The Heart of Jesus is a spring of purity, love and suffering. Infinite Love is purity, and when that Love came to earth to purify it, this Love became suffering, so that from the innermost recesses of that Love purity might break forth for our souls.

Ah, this Divine Love, which cannot be defined nor expressed, but which we experience without understanding it, is in that Divine Heart, which suffers deep wounds of love. Which moves, astounds and fascinates one, driving one crazy with the foolishness of the cross. O delights of Divine Love that surpass all earthly delights! O most loving and Sorrowful Heart of Jesus! May You be blessed!

This Divine Heart wants to unite Itself to us in an intimate embrace and to fuse our soul into His Own. He loves us in order to reveal His secrets to us. To grant us His Spirit. To give us that which is His. To inebriate us with His love and to communicate to us His very Life, His heartbeats, His martyrdoms and His happiness.

Prayer

Dear Jesus, I want to help You with Your interior cross. I want You to share with me some of those intimate, bitter sufferings that hurt You so much. I want to be pure for those who are not pure. I want to sacrifice myself for those who do not sacrifice themselves. To be grateful for the ungrateful. To be Your victim on behalf of Your beloved Church.

O Mary, Jesus' life came to an end on Calvary, but His interior Passion continued in your heart until it also died whenever it contemplated Jesus' sacrifice. You left upon earth an example that other hearts would later imitate. We are not worthy, but we place our souls into your hands so that you might pour into them at least a little of Jesus' bitter sufferings. Amen.

7

HIS SOUL

"Who is the refulgence of His glory,
the very imprint of His being, and Who sustains
all things by His mighty word.

When He had accomplished purification
from sins, He took His seat at the right hand
of the Majesty on high" (cf. Heb 1:3).

Jesus' most pure soul was like a shining crystal without stain. Like a burst of light. Like a peaceful lake. Like an impeccable mirror reflecting divinity itself.

"Who of you can charge Me of sin?" (Jn 8: 46), Jesus said in all truth because no one could be purer than He could. His most pure soul gives brilliance to the snow, whiteness to the lily, makes things diaphanous transparent. It reflects the heaven of the Divinity in its most pure depths.

One must climb the Cross and see heaven

and earth through Jesus' eyes, wherein His soul radiated all transparency. If we want to know what Jesus is like we, like Him, must offer ourselves, without blemish, to God through the Holy Spirit. With the light of the wisdom of the Cross, we will come to know Him.

Jesus' most pure soul suffered all the pains, thorns and the bitterness and more, which we don't even suspect and which chosen souls whom He has made participants of His intimate sufferings barely glimpse.

Jesus' suffering was totally unique, since it was brought about by a single Love. It is impossible for us to really understand every aspect of that unique suffering. It is something deep and incomprehensible when one sees Divine Glory attacked. It is tender compassion when He seeks out wayward souls. It is wounded goodness caused by ingratitude. It is being torn asunder by sins. It is torture because of rebellious souls; bitter tears for insensitive souls; bitterness without hope; impotent anxiety; pieces torn from His soul when souls definitively separate themselves from His love and His life.

Let us imagine a reservoir that would gather and capture all the springs of earth... a conflagration that would join together all the fires of all the suns... a light which would concentrate the splendor of all the stars. What must have been the suffering of Jesus' soul Who, in His Divine Unity, concentrated all the springs of suffering and all the perfection of love? O most holy soul of Jesus — sanctify us!

Prayer

O sorrowful Mary, Mother who suffered in tune with Jesus' soul, even though I am unworthy, unite me to Him, because of the love and suffering which martyred Jesus' sinless soul. Amen.

8

HIS TWO LOVES

"My sheep hear My voice; I know them, and they follow Me. I give them eternal life, and they shall never perish. No one can take them out of My hand. My Father, who has given them to Me, is greater than all, and no one can take them out of the Father's hand" (cf. Jn 10:27-29).

His Father and souls! These were Jesus' constant concerns, His dominant passions, so to say, His sublime loves. Ever forgetful of Himself, before anything else He sought to fulfill the most Holy Will of His beloved Father. He also sought after the lost sheep until He was able to place it on His shoulders so that He could return it to its Master.

Jesus was always seeking the glory of His Father. *"I do not seek My own glory,"* He said, *"I honor My Father and I always do what is pleasing to Him"* (cf. Jn 8:50).

In Jesus, there was such an admirable subordination to the Divine Will of His Father, in Whom He lived absorbed! His Heart was consumed with desire as it burned in holy zeal for the salvation of souls. For thirty years, He held this within Himself, until there arrived the hour destined by the Father for His apostolate. *"My hour has not yet arrived"* (cf. Jn. 7:6), He would say. But His Heart burned with love for us in His concern for our salvation.

You have told me that You have loved me in the way that the Father loved You. That is the reason for Your knowing how to love with such tenderness. With such forgetfulness of self. With such faithfulness as no one else has ever loved me. If Your commandment is that we love our neighbor as Your Father has loved You, how are we to love You so as to respond to that incomparable tenderness?

Jesus loves us with the same love with which He loves His Father and with which His Father has loved Him. *"As the Father has loved Me, so I have loved you"* (Jn 15:9). Can one imagine a greater love for souls? We must love others in the same way.

Should we love souls only on the condition that they love us? No. That is not God's way. We must love others in spite of all ingratitude, in spite of all betrayals, in spite of the poverty of the human heart. With a love that, transcending time, goes to lose itself in the immensity of God. Such is Jesus' love. Jesus is like that.

People who come into our lives are as pieces of canvas on which we must paint the image of Jesus. We are to think that what we do for them, we are doing for Him. We are never to believe ourselves offended. When we feel our heart wounded, instead of resentments springing from it, let there only pour out of it the cool water of prayers and the blood of our sacrifices for them.

Prayer

You, Mary, who loved the eternal Father with a flame so intense that you could not live except in accordance with His adorable Will, please grant us your fidelity and your generosity of soul, so that we might embrace its dispositions even should they sacrifice us and that we might use all the strength of our hearts in loving Him and in giving Him thousands of souls who might love Him. Amen.

9

HIS LOVE FOR SOULS

"As the Father loves Me, so I also I have loved you"
(cf. Jn 15:9).

How does Jesus love us? He loves us with the same love with which He loves His heavenly Father: that is, with the Holy Spirit. We could never have dreamt that we might be loved in this manner, the way Jesus loves us, participating in the very love with which Jesus loves the Father. Who would be able to comprehend this?

In this love with which Jesus loves us is the very Love in which the thrice holy God burns. It is an efficacious, fruitful love. An unquenchable Fount of blessings. He pours forth this love into us with incomprehensible generosity. A love solely conceived and perpetuated by God Himself.

We want a love, ever ancient, from before we existed. We want to taste and feel the words of Isaiah 54:8, *"I have loved you with an everlasting love."* There has never been a single instant when we have not been loved by that love.

The love of Jesus is superior to the wildest dreams or desires of our souls because, besides being inexhaustible, it is unique and it possesses at the same time all of the loves that have ever existed. In the Heart of Jesus we find the tender love of a mother, the generous love of a father, the sweet love of a spouse, the intimate love of a friend and a great deal more that we cannot begin to find the human words to explain.

This mysterious love is unique not only because it excludes the frailty of other loves while containing all their beauty, but it is also unique because it adapts perfectly to each soul and assumes in each one, as it were, that soul's form.

And if we wish, we can fully enjoy that unending and rich love without fear of losing it. To the degree that we can penetrate into this love of Jesus — into that ocean of love — the greater assurance we will have that we shall never leave its scope. *"Who can separate me from the love of Christ?"* (cf. Rm 8:35).

For our part, the Love which the Holy Spirit diffuses in our hearts is of itself permanent, because it is Life. Of course, we can lose this Love by our sins, but only if we want to. Anyway, who, having known Jesus, would want to offend Him?

Whoever loves Jesus in spirit and in truth thinks that he or she will always love Him. It is only this kind of love that attains the ideal Love — the ultimate desire of all love. It is Love itself that is the greatest reward of true love.

Also, the human heart expands in the ocean of Infinite Love: a love that is infinite, ever new, deep as the ocean, immense as the heavens! Who would ever imagine that we might be the object of that profoundly intense love of Jesus? His love is an infinite gift: the fullness of all goodness, perfection and beauty.

Although that love which Jesus has placed in the soul is so intense, this soul perceives it as nothing compared to the love that Jesus deserves. One attempts to love in a new way and feels the paucity of that love and does not know which is sweeter: the new love which sets the soul on fire, or the strange enchantment of feeling totally impotent to respond to the love which envelops it.

Has Jesus ever forgotten us? Or has He perchance lied to us? Has He not fulfilled each of His promises with divine generosity? Has He not surpassed all the illusions and dreams of our hearts for His glory?

Prayer

O Mary! O Mother of beautiful Love! You lived and breathed with His breath and you focused all your tenderness on Him! May I love Him more and more each day, as you do. Given that love without works is not true love, grant, Mary, that I may prove my love by my generous sacrifice. I want to be like you, my Mother. I want to generously give myself over to sacrifice out of pure love. Amen.

10

LOVING COMPLAINTS

*"Have I been with you for so long a time
and you still do not know Me, Philip?"
(cf. Jn 14:9).*

From His monstrance, from His tabernacle,
from the depth of our hearts, He speaks to us.
"For such a long time I have been with you, living by your side, coming to you daily in Holy
Communion, never leaving you, being even
closer than I was to My disciples. Still you do
not know Me? Have you not contemplated My
virtues? Have you not entered into My Sacred
Heart? Have you not shared My very Life? I love
you so much, so very much, beloved soul who
is listening to Me."

That emotion of Jesus as He delicately ren-
ders His most tender complaints. That emotion
— that causes our being to come to life even after so many centuries — came from the depths

of the Infinite, the Sublime and the Divine. Jesus was deeply moved and He was speaking to all the cold and indifferent souls of all the ages with the emphasis of the heart.

Again Jesus, Whom we so frequently forget about, complains with a sadness that tears the heart about that which hurts Him most: our ingratitude! This dagger thrust is terrible for a noble Heart, Who has only known how to pour forth blessings. For what must the most sensitive, the most pure and loving Heart, have felt when being forgotten by His children? What a painful sword being forgotten is for the Soul Who only knew how to love and to sacrifice Himself in every form of martyrdom to bring happiness to those He loves!

We really do not comprehend the profound Love that the Heart of Jesus has for us. The more Jesus deigns to reveal to us those secrets of His loving Heart, the more we realize that we do not understand Him.

His Infinite Love causes Him to complain on the one hand, while our littleness inclines Him to forgive us. It is only our misery that draws God toward us, because that is all that is ours. It is into this emptiness — into this nothingness — that the ocean of His Goodness and the Infinite Love of His Heart are poured.

In order to love Jesus, we must know Him. We must think about Him. Live from His life as a Victim. Taste Him, analyze Him, study Him and understand Him. We must discover Him and live intimately united to Him. As moss is to the tree. As the branch is to the vine. As light is to the sun. It is to imitate Him and live His life, docile to His action, trying to fulfill the least of His wishes. Sacrificing everything in order to please Him.

His Divine Heart is like a hearth of charity that loves and wants to be loved. His delight consists in diffusing Himself, in giving Himself, in communicating Himself to us and in making us happy. Jesus is like that!

His Most Sacred Heart is a divine furnace that invites us to lovingly immolate our souls in union with Him for the salvation of souls.

Jesus is like that! All love in order to set the universe on fire. All the sufferings of His body and soul, of His mind and His senses, were concentrated in His Heart. But the more intense ones, those without measure, were not produced by the nails, the scourging, the thorns, or the lance, but by our sins and ingratitude.

Prayer

Mary, my Mother! I know that the one who is best able to love is the one who best knows how to voluntarily suffer, the better in order to console you. Mother of my soul, grant that I may never bring sadness to Jesus' Heart by my forgetfulness of Him and my ingratitude. Grant that I might know Him, meditate upon Him, penetrate Him and that He may never be able to complain about my not loving Him enough. I do love Him so very much! Amen.

11

HIS APOSTOLATE

*"The Spirit of the Lord is upon Me, because He has
anointed Me to bring glad tidings to the poor.
He has sent Me to proclaim liberty to captives and
recovery of sight to the blind, to let the oppressed
go free, and to proclaim a year acceptable
to the Lord" (cf. Lk 4:18-19).*

In His earthly life and especially during His pub-
lic life, Jesus was always in contact with people.
From this interaction, He suffered things that
very few people really think about and which
hardly anyone understands.

The gospel tells us that His very own did
not believe in Him (Jn 6:64). Every single one
of us belongs to Jesus. We are His. With regard
to each one of us, Jesus felt our personal struggle
in His Heart: that of the Love which urged Him
on toward us and that of our sins, which caused
Him to suffer.

How did Jesus begin His apostolate? He began it by leaving Mary behind. What a tremendous farewell! He had to tear Himself from the sum and substance of His love because His hour had come — the hour for Him to sacrifice Himself and save us. He was going to cast Himself into the sea of persecution and hatred — a road of suffering — knowing that it would end in His being nailed to the cross, His infinite tenderness not having been understood!

To show us how we should prepare for our own apostolate, Jesus began with a humbling experience that moved heaven itself. He went to the Jordan River to be baptized as though He were a sinner. He Who was innocence without blemish — the Incarnate Word — the God-Man! He fasted for forty days in the desert and began His apostolic life like this: with humility and penance, giving us an example to be imitated.

Infinite Love knew how to live by love, but He did not know how to die of love. On Calvary He understood and experienced the wisdom of the cross. He satisfied His thirst to suffer for our sake and at the same time, He showed us the way to heaven.

Jesus diffuses love because He is Infinite Goodness. If we love Him, we can't keep it stored away in the inner recesses of our soul. Wonder of wonders! The more we give of Jesus, the more we actually possess Him. It is enough to know Him and love Him in order to give Him. Divinity is fullness — and all fullness overflows. Just as God, by giving Himself, not only makes His creatures happy, but at the same time glorifies Himself, when the soul of the apostle gives Jesus to others, he makes souls happy and he is giving Jesus souls who will glorify Him.

It is the nature of God to give Himself and He communicates this divine inclination to those who love Him. When we give Him to others, we bring joy to Jesus' Heart with souls who will love Him. In giving Him, we give glory to the Father and we cooperate with the outpouring of the love of the Holy Spirit. Thus we shall possess Him more intimately and we shall also love Him with the hearts that we give Him.

We draw near to souls through the written word, through advice, through serving one another, and through teachings. If we have a true love for souls, Jesus will put us in contact with them. Then our duty is to never refuse any sacrifice, either of body or soul, no matter what it might cost us. Are we suffering? Happy the trial that achieves grace! We should accept with a smile those circumstances that evoke sacrifice. Should we not reproduce the mystery of Christ in His apostolate?

Goodness is the vengeance of great souls. Let us go forward! For faith and love shall overcome all failings and acts of ingratitude and when we are trying to glorify God, all martyrdoms shall seem sweet.

Prayer

Mary, you who were and are the universal instrument of the action which Jesus realizes in our souls, help us. It was the will of Jesus that you should be the Co-Redemptrix of the human race because of your love and sacrifices and that you should be the Mediatrix of all graces, in Him and through Him. Amen.

12

HIS WORDS

*"Master, to whom shall we go? You have the
words of eternal life" (cf. Jn 6:68).*

Heavenly words of mercy, of justice, of sublime
charity and of holy love fell from the divine lips
of Jesus as gentle dew falling upon a parched
earth.

His words were — and continue to be
— the great Splendor, the great Light for all
mankind. His lips always spoke piety, sweetness
and confidence. He was and is Goodness, Mercy
and Kindness personified.

If we were to allow His words to penetrate
our hearts, how rapidly we would begin our
transformation into Him and the truth is that
by our good fortune, Jesus lives in our souls and
suffers in us.

Who has ever said that the presence of God
— in His actions and His words — has to be
felt? Sometimes God grants that sensation. At

other times, He doesn't. But having or not having that disposition does not necessarily mean that we are far from God.

When one comes to understand this, one receives desolation — the inability to hear Jesus' voice interiorly — as a precious grace from God and one accepts it in peace.

There will be periods of dryness, lack of consolation, fatigue and struggles. But in the midst of this, just as when we feel fervor, the same love must continue burning: a love that adapts itself to all circumstances and is never extinguished. This love comes from God and that which is divine is also immortal.

The words of Jesus enthrall us and fill us with love. In them we find all that is pure, luminous and beautiful and they take the soul beyond one's possible dreams of holiness. Those words of Jesus are food, light, perfume, life, delight, strength and love!

"Let anyone who thirsts come to Me and drink" (cf. Jn 7:37). In the world of souls, oh Jesus, we are dying of thirst because we have strayed away from You, Who are the fountain of life! *"Give us that water,"* we say today with the Samaritan woman. Give us to drink from that Heart, which is a divine wellspring of life that will flow without ceasing, even to eternal life.

O Jesus, why do we not meditate daily

upon Your Divine Words, where You throb with all the tenderness of Your Infinite Love?

Jesus is the Ocean that overflows in His gospel. He has an infinite desire that we meditate upon and apply His words. He wants to give Himself to us. His greatest joy is to find souls open to receive His gifts. Expansive and open souls into whom He can pour His gifts in the sure knowledge that all will be welcomed, even when these gifts bring bitterness and suffering.

Prayer

O Jesus, Your gospel is Your very life among us! It is You Who came to earth that we might have life and *"life in abundance"* (Jn 10:10). Your doctrine is my breath, my drink and the light that brings joy to my eyes. Your words are my strength in my struggles. My rest, my peace, my best companions and my reward. This is because You are there. The Doctor Who knows me and Who cures my every ailment. The Shepherd Who guides me as His beloved sheep. The King Whom I serve. The Friend from Whom I hold nothing back. The Husband Whom I worship. He Who has the remedy for every disorder. The Divine Word Himself. The Splendor of the Father, of His holiness and of His beauty. Amen.

13

HIS GAZE

"Jesus, looking at him, loved him"
(cf. Mk 10:21).

Jesus' gaze, when He walked the earth, would cause a profound awakening in others. When He passed by, the eyes of the blind were opened. Paralytics threw away their crutches. Those who were sick sprang from their beds completely cured. Jesus had a divine attraction about Him which tore at hearts that were thirsting for love and truth. He satisfied their longing because He Himself was Love, Truth and Life.

Jesus always looks at us with Infinite Kindness. He watches over us. He never tires of knocking at the door of our hearts. Nor does He tire of waiting for us to open to Him, because He loves us. He will take our mortal life into His own divine hands so that He might give us eternal life. He will close our eyes here on earth, that He might open them to the True Light. He will always be our consolation and our happiness. He will not allow us to weep like those who have no hope.

The Father looks with a glance that gives. We, on the other hand, look with an attitude of seeking. We look asking for things. By means of that Eternal and Infinite Gaze, the Father communicated His essence to the Divine Word. That Gaze is life-giving, since it is the gaze of God Himself. The soul is a mirror in which the Divine Gaze is reflected. God is light. The more this Divine Light shines, the greater the union we will have. The greater the innocence and purity of heart. Then, if Jesus looks at us, we shall also contemplate Him because He has said, *"Blessed are the pure of heart, for they shall see God"* (cf. Mt 5:8).

Let us ask Jesus to look at us as He looked at St. Peter. As He looked at Mary Magdalene. With this life-giving gaze that produces saints. Let us beg for those Divine Glances that open the soul to holy expansiveness. And let us allow ourselves to be bathed in those Most Holy Glances that purify, sanctify, unite and intimately bind the Divine Heart to our own.

Jesus wishes that His Eternal Gaze at His Father pass on through our souls and our eyes. His is a Gaze of purity, tenderness and adoration. Let us always keep our eyes fixed on Jesus, that we may know Him, discern His desires, better understand His teachings and penetrate into His Heart.

In that Gaze, Jesus would put His love, His surrender, His tenderness and His complete abandonment to the will of the Father: in a word, His entire soul. All that is in Jesus had, as its source and origin, that Divine and Intimate Gaze at His Father. This radiated in His person and was reflected in His words and in the wonders that He performed.

Let us also look at the Father unceasingly, as Jesus did, with a Gaze of purity, adoration, surrender and abandonment. Let us place all our lives into His Gaze and let us ask Jesus to look at His Father through the eyes of our soul.

Let us imitate Jesus in His Gaze. Always tender, sweet and loving. Ever the same, whether at the Last Supper or at Gethsemane. Let us also see the Father in all of creation, in the beauty of nature. But especially, let us see Him in souls, because His Divine Image is reflected in them better than in the blue of the skies or the waves of the sea.

Prayer

Lord, is it not true that Your Gaze is Love? That Your heaven is love and that my longing to see You is a reflection of Your promise of eternal life? You saw that I was lost and You came to look for me. You saw that, without Your help, I would be unable to go to You. So You came to look for me. How marvelous is the Infinite Love of our God! Amen.

14

HIS CHARITY

"Come to Me, all you who labor and are burdened, and I will give you rest" (Mt 11:28).

"My son, give Me your heart" (Pr 23:26). This is why Jesus came into this world: He wanted to be loved by us. He wanted to seek out the hearts that would love Him, so that He might offer them to His heavenly Father.

His love is the sum of all perfection, the summation of all the virtues; it is the holy life. Our lives should have a goal: Love itself. God's love is as strong as death. It has wings immaculate as those of a dove and strong as those of an eagle to take us away from the miseries of earth and lift us up to the regions of Infinite Happiness.

Jesus' thirst is insatiable. Its depths are unfathomable. He loves and desires to be loved. He loves and, in His Sovereign Humility, wants us to let ourselves be loved by Him. There are many souls who love Him, but only a few who allow themselves to be loved by Him. Even more, He wants us to ask Him to love us.

Love has many dimensions, but let us consider only three of them. The first is to love Jesus with our whole heart, our whole soul, with all our strength and with the tenderness, fidelity, sensitivity and nobility of true love.

The second dimension is to let ourselves be loved by Jesus. What do we mean by "letting ourselves be loved by Him"? It is to receive His approach of love even if it annihilates us and embarrasses us. Letting ourselves be loved by Him is to open ourselves to all the demands of love. It is to give Jesus pleasure in His most intimate desires.

It means looking at Him when He wants us to look at Him. It means loving Him as He wants us to love Him. It means being silent when He needs us to be silent. It means speaking when He is listening. Listening when He is speaking. Being in spiritual darkness when this pleases Him and enjoying His light when He sends it.

In a word, letting ourselves be loved means losing our soul in Jesus and being a flawless mirror that reflects His Glance. It means being flexible to His will as if our own had neither life nor being, except that of receiving His love and accommodating ourselves to His desires. Jesus respects the will of the creature and holds back at the doors of our heart, waiting for us to open them to Him.

And what is the other dimension of love? It consists not only in loving — not only in allowing ourselves to be loved — but in the soul forgetting itself totally, thinking only about pleasing the Beloved. Casting itself into His arms as did the bride of the Canticle of Canticles, asking to be loved by Him: *"Kiss me with the kiss of Your mouth"* (cf. Sg 1:2).

Those who have reached the heights of humility know that their weaknesses do not impede God's work. They open their hearts to receive the Divine Graces, to respond to them and enjoy them because they are centered upon God and not upon themselves.

In this type of love, the soul imitates Jesus in His desire to be loved. He had that dimension of love in all its ineffable fullness. For this He came into the world: to seek our love. The souls who ask for His caresses have eyes only for God, Who seems to them as infinitely good. Their trust has grown because they have disappeared — having died to self in order to live in God. Jesus loves us with a divine craziness. He is blinded by His love for us.

In loving us, He still sees our weaknesses, but He covers them with the reflection of His own beauty. He sees the depths of our miseries and nothingness, but He has the Almighty virtue to place the treasure of His mercy in them. For He knows how to draw wonders of beauty out of chaos. This is Jesus. Jesus is like that.

Prayer

O Mary, finest model of perfect charity and Mother of beautiful Love! Imprint in our hearts all the traits of holy love. May the Divine Fire in which your heart burns be communicated to our hearts, for we long to be inflamed and be consumed as incense for the glory of God and Jesus' consolation. Grant that we might understand the Divine Sweetness of union with God. With you, may we form a single heart and a single soul, so that we never desire, nor enjoy, nor love anything outside of Jesus. Amen.

15

HIS GOODNESS

"Jesus went about doing good and healing all those oppressed by the devil, for God was with Him"
(Acts 10:38).

Following Jesus means nothing other than re-producing His virtues in ourselves, in order to do all things well. It is trying to assume His imprint on our bodies and our souls that we might be entirely transformed into Him.

Jesus is resolved to captivate our hearts, for as Holy Scripture says, He is "totally attractive": totally genial, fascinating, sensitive, and divine. He passed through this world doing good. He did all things well.

He cannot see suffering without being compassionate. Wherever He finds pain, He consoles and brings sweetness to the suffering, as much in His earthly life as in the Holy Eucharist, because the Heart of Jesus does not change.

The Good Shepherd, He says, knows His sheep and He is pleased that they know Him (cf. Jn 10:14). *"I have other sheep,"* He says, *"but that one grieves Me, and I want it to return to My fold."* He would welcome sinners and He would be all things to all men.

When one strikes a harp, it responds only with harmony. When petals are removed from a flower, it gives its best perfume. The good soul is both a harp and a flower. When it is wounded by criticism and torn apart by ingratitude, it can only respond with harmony and the perfume of goodness. How beautiful are the souls that seem to pulsate with self-sacrifice and with kindness!

True humility does not notice the faults and failings of one's neighbor. True charity does not make them known. Goodness forgives them.

His obedience was even to the point of death on the cross in order to save us. His mortification subjected Him to the grind of everyday work. His zeal moved Him to go from town to town healing the sick, consoling, teaching — becoming all things for all men. That is our model.

This is Jesus! The One Who went about doing good. People would say, *"Goodness itself has appeared in our midst."* And we have that Goodness — that crucified Jesus — within our grasp in the Holy Eucharist and in our hearts.

What was the characteristic which influenced all His actions, the distinctive attribute of His spirit, the ultimate quality in which He was most outstanding? It was the cross, self-sacrifice and self-immolation!

Jesus here poses the spirit of self-renunciation and mortification as the indispensable condition for following Him, for imitating Him, for going through this world performing good works. He invites us to taste the sweet pain of a life of voluntary sacrifice, in union with Him.

Prayer

O Mary, good Mother, make me yours. You who are all amiability and deference. Your glance is a soothing balm for my wounds and your heart a spring offering. A never-ending hope. You are the mother of those who suffer and those who weep. You are kindness. You are tenderness. At your side, sufferings become sweet and where there are anxieties to calm and tears to wipe, you are there, Mary — all sweetness — and full of compassion. Amen.

16

HIS TENDERNESS

"How many times I yearned to gather your children together, as a hen gathers her young under her wings" (Mt 23:37).

The Heart of Jesus longs for an intimate love with souls and He rejoices when He finds another heart with whom He might freely have it. Furthermore, the purer, humbler and more self-sacrificing this heart is, the more complete His joy will be.

In His dealing with souls, Jesus showed — and still shows — unbelievable tenderness. He is tenderness personified! He is the most loving Son of the Father Whose desire is to give Himself, to pour Himself out in graces and charisms. He agreed to redeem man that He might infuse into him the torrent of grace and love of which He is the Fount.

Jesus is so tender and compassionate that

He is concerned about putting out the smoldering wick or breaking the bruised reed, or hurting any soul. Jesus is always waiting for the sinner and He is deeply hurt by the ingratitude of men and women. But He loves them and shows His mercy, pardoning their weaknesses by offering the price of His blood to His heavenly Father.

What would we on earth do without Jesus? Who would be equivalent to Him to love us, seek us, wait for us, or pardon us?

Jesus, look upon us with all of Your tenderness. Repair the damage that sin has caused in our souls. See what weakness our heart bears. How easily we turn to evil! How lukewarm we are! Please deign to come and help us. I know that all that really belongs to us is our human weakness. But these very weaknesses draw You so that You might remedy them. For they are the emptiness — the hollow spaces — into which the ocean of Your Goodness is poured.

What happiness it is to give to Jesus what He asks of us — what He wants — whether it is love or suffering! Would that our love was truly pure, for then it would be more advantageous and more meritorious than all our actions, which are tainted by self-love.

Do we really wish to plunge into the depths

of tenderness of the Divine Heart of Jesus? Let us remember His tears, my God, because Jesus wept when He was on earth. This earth was watered and purified by the tender tears of that loving Heart.

Blessed be the tears of Jesus that purchased heaven for us! Creative tears! Tears that washed away the iniquities of earth. Tears that have been perpetuated in the wellsprings of the Holy Sacraments! O compassionate Jesus, Who forgives everything and forgets it and Who reaches out His arms to us! Wash us with Your tears and cleanse us with Your Divine Blood!

We beseech You for so many hearts whom we love and for our own hearts, so full of human judgments, lazy in the practice of virtue and drawn by the pleasures of the world. We pray for those who tend more to pampering themselves than to fervor and self-sacrifice. Come Jesus, cure our tepidity, warm the coldness of our hearts and do away with our indifference.

Let us wipe away those pearls from His Divine Eyes with our love and offer Him many converted souls to console Him.

Prayer

Jesus, we want to empty our life into You. We want to be able to pour all of our tenderness into Your Heart. We want to be consumed by Its fire, as a holocaust for love of You. We will no longer hesitate to make any sacrifice. Give us, O Lord, that union with You that we so desire. Give us a love for You that is so pure, so holy, so devoid of self-love, so full of charity toward our neighbor and so much Your own that we will only concern ourselves with pleasing You and consoling You. Amen.

17

HIS COMPASSION

"When He disembarked and saw the vast crowd,
His heart was moved with pity for them,
for they were like sheep without a shepherd"
(Mk 6:34).

Jesus was not able to see suffering without His
Heart being touched and feeling sympathy,
ever consoling the one who suffers and making the pain His own. Jesus could not see tears
in another person's eyes without wiping them,
because the compassion of the God-Man is always aroused by our pain, a pain He feels in the
intimate depths of His Heart.

In regard to the Samaritan woman, He
arranges it so that He is the One encountered
and He waits for her at Jacob's well to convert
her. His Compassionate Heart suffers when He
sees souls in sin. Jesus waits untiringly for the
conversion of sinners.

Weary, Jesus waits. His body is thirsty, but His Heart thirsts even more. He is exhausted from His apostolic endeavors. He sits with infinite patience — waiting — just as He waits for us, despite our blameworthy abuses of His Goodness.

Jesus is not thinking about His physical hunger because *"His food is to do the will of His heavenly Father"* (Jn 4:34).

What was His reaction to the woman taken in adultery? He told her that although everyone had condemned her, He would not do so. His compassion brought Him to put into play both His Almighty Power and His Goodness. With what gentleness and tenderness He tells the adulterous woman, *"Go now and sin no more"* (Jn 8:11). He sends her away free from her enemies.

He would forget about Himself to think about those whom He loved and also about those who despised Him. He would not be content with revealing Himself to us, with unveiling His Compassionate Heart. He also would give us the secret of obtaining from God all that we might want, if it were not to our detriment. *"Ask and you shall receive,"* He would say. *"Knock and it shall be opened to you. Until now you have never asked the Father for anything in My name"* (Mt 7:7; Jn 16:24). Ask, ask!

Let us now look at our own hearts. How many times do we fail in charity toward our neighbor, toward those very ones with whom we live and work. And why? Because of the hardness of our hearts. Because of our self-centeredness. Because we don't want to be bothered with serving them. Because we are so preoccupied with our own pleasures, affairs and comforts that we are not moved by the needs of others.

How would Jesus look at these people? How should we be looking at them? How? We should look at them through the eyes of Jesus. If we did this, how much compassion, goodness, and love we would feel for them! Let us expand our soul so that Jesus might fill it to a greater and greater degree and might infuse into us His own Compassion toward our neighbor. It is so pleasant to do good! There are three things that expand the soul: purity, sacrifice and love. Is it possible that these three things could be, as it were, a reflection of the Blessed Trinity?

Let us love others with the Ultimate Love — with the Holy Spirit Himself. It is not the same to love with a single ray of the sun as to love with the sun itself. The absolute perfection of the virtue of charity is to love with the Holy Spirit. To love our neighbor with the Holy Spirit is to love him as God loves Himself and as He loves us.

May all that we see, whether in heaven or on earth, speak to us of love, re-echo love, impregnating us with holy love toward our neighbor, and may we put into practice all the works of mercy in His regard.

Prayer

O loving Mother, please obtain for me a true forgetfulness of myself and a loving and heroic compassion for Jesus' Heart and for your own Heart. Amen.

18

HIS MERCY

*"Be compassionate just as your heavenly Father is
compassionate. Do not judge others and you will not
be judged; pardon and you will be pardoned.
Give and it will be given to you" (Lk 6:36).*

We need not do a great deal of thinking to appreciate what Jesus has been for us! We need only recall some of the happy memories of our lives and, full of gratitude and love, we shall realize some of what we owe Him.

How much He has loved us at every stage and at every moment of our lives!

With what ineffable gentleness He has treated us!

With what patience He has endured us!

With what solicitude He has cared for us!

With what tenderness He has led us, not by the hand, but in His arms and in His Heart!

What finesse He has shown us!

This is how Jesus is! This is His Infinite Charity. This is the way He knows how to love us: unmindful of our sins, casting our infidelities into the sea, drowning our unfaithfulness in the wellspring of the Love of His Heart, consuming even the straws of our imperfections in the fire of His bosom.

We, on the other hand — in our shame — should we not try to clothe ourselves with the loving kindness of our Model Jesus?

O how different are our hearts from the Merciful Heart of Jesus! He is so good and holy. So humble and so loving! Jesus' thoughts are so lofty and pure! His affection is so profound and sincere! His speech is so charitable that His words seem to cover our defects and deficiencies! His words are overflowing with Truth, Light and Love! His deeds are so good and so heavenly! That is Jesus. Jesus is like that!

How different earthly love is when compared to the love of Jesus! We have the assurance that He loves us despite the fact that He knows our lack of beauty and our deficiencies. With the clearest Light, He sees us as we are and this is the way He loves us. He loves us because we are weak and small! How fortunate we are that this is the way He is. His love, which is Infinite Light, sees us and loves us just the way we are.

God's grace is not measured by what we are. Nor is it given in proportion to our merits.

Undoubtedly, there is such an admirable contrast between our littleness and God's generosity. God grants His grace to souls not because they merit it, but because He wants to.

Prayer

And you, Mary, who are all pure, loving, and indulgent, whose Heart burns with love for souls, obtain for us the grace to be truly grateful to your Son. This we beg of you, our most loving Mother of Mercy.

19

HIS SILENCE

"The chief priests accused Him of many things. Again Pilate questioned Him, 'Have you no answer? See how many things they accuse you of.' Jesus gave him no further answer" (Mk 15:4-5).

Jesus gave us truly heroic examples of silence even in the most painful stages of His life. They insulted Him. They slapped Him in the face and He, with infinite sweetness, only asks, *"If I speak the truth, why do you strike Me?"* (Jn 18:23).

They slandered Him, they accused Him and they told Him that He was in league with the devil. But He responded only with an admirable silence. They called him a "Samaritan," a blasphemer and a seducer of the people. He remained silent in order to show us how to remain silent when we are unjustly accused or insulted.

Jesus kept silent for thirty years, even though His Heart longed to save souls. He remained silent until the moment arrived that had been indicated by the Divine Will of His heavenly Father.

We, too, should live our lives eclipsed in God, hidden within Him. When He wishes, He will sacrifice us or He will fill us with consolations, not separating us from Him, but uniting us to Him. Exteriorly, we may have to pass through all the vicissitudes of life, but interiorly, we should live with our eyes fixed upon Jesus, united to Jesus, with no other life outside of His Life and with no other love than His Love.

If Jesus seems to be silent, we already know that just as His words are divine, so are His silences, because they are His. If Jesus is Faithfulness itself, He does not know how to abandon anyone. It is we souls who withdraw from Him, not He Who leaves us. When He is silent, when He is hidden, it is because it is better for us. When He seems to be in hiding, He is uniting Himself most intimately with our souls.

Silence is the most intimate part of God. We may hear no human words, but the silence itself is vibrant and eloquent. It is a silence in which all things are spoken. In which everything is understood. In which everything is light, peace, order, and love. In that Divine Silence, souls understand more than in the communications of a lesser order.

It was in the Divine Silence that creation took place. In this silence we were redeemed and the Church and the sacraments were instituted. God rejoices in the harmonious concert of all that has been created and that shall be created, because He has produced all of it Himself. He is the Cause of all causes and the Infinite and Eternal Origin of all that is pure and holy.

The divine fruitfulness of the most Blessed Trinity in every soul, in the Church and in all creation is actualized within the deep, profound, Divine Silence of God. When He wishes to elevate souls to His Divinity, He surrounds them and imbues them in that Eternal Silence, that there they might study and understand, insofar as it might be possible, what Jesus is really like.

Let us love Jesus unconditionally in every circumstance of life, so that we might vanish and He might think, be silent, speak and work in us.

Prayer

Mary, you are the Silent Virgin, who lived absorbed, contemplating in Jesus the secrets of heaven. Obtain for us that interior life of union with Him, in order to hear the divine inspirations of the Holy Spirit.

O Mary, Beloved Virgin, how were you able to keep the divine treasure of that Heavenly Fire in your soul and in your heart without melting? If Jesus burned with this fire, why were your virginal body and your most holy soul not consumed?

To me, your life is like that prodigy that Moses contemplated in the desert. You were a bush that burned with an immense flame for many long years without being consumed — until, at last, one happy day, the Divine Fire consumed you. Please grant us a little spark of that Divine Fire, that we might live in love and that we might die of love. Amen.

20

HIS POVERTY

"And she gave birth to her firstborn son.
She wrapped Him in swaddling clothes and laid
Him in a manger, because there was no room
for them in the inn" (Lk 2:7).

What can we say about Jesus' voluntary poverty?
Although He is the Lord and Master of heaven
and earth, He descended to earth, leaving behind His throne above the Seraphim, to be born
in a manger for animals, at midnight, trembling
with cold upon some straw — all this for love
of us.

"Seek first the kingdom of God and His justice,
and everything else will be given to you" (Mt 6:33).
If we seek the kingdom of heaven, we will have
everything else. Let us live of Him alone. May
Jesus be our wealth and our only treasure. May
His love be our only possession.

He was born poor, He was brought up poor

and He lived in a humble home. Jesus accepted all forms of poverty as His companions and He always lived among humble people. It was from among poor fishermen that He chose the disciples that were to convert the world.

Before dying, Jesus even wanted to give us His Blessed Mother. Who but Jesus could give His very mother to us for our joy and happiness? Have we at least once adequately appreciated this benevolent generosity? Have we at least once stopped to consider it?

This is Jesus, the embodiment of love and tenderness, ever forgetful of self and remembering us, that we might be blessed. But what am I saying? He even surrendered His own Body. He dispossessed Himself of His Most Holy Flesh and His own Precious Blood, to leave it to us so that we might be nourished by this heavenly food until the end of time.

He was aware of all the horrors that awaited Him in the Holy Eucharist: rejections, sacrileges, ingratitude and even hellish wrath against this Sacrament of Divine Love. But the love of the Heart of Jesus rose above all of this. Constant in His love for us, He was indifferent to poverty and insults as long as we might be blessed, might place His Heart in our heart daily in Holy Communion, and He might be our very food and life.

Let us study this Model of voluntary poverty. This Jesus, Who was poor throughout His life and Who remains poor in the Eucharist. There we have the Jesus of Bethlehem, of Nazareth and of the cross! There He is, He Who has even surrendered the capacity to move, without the least radiance that might signal His Presence. There He laments the abandonment even of those who are His own!

How can we remove from Jesus this paucity of love? How can we mitigate that poverty, which makes Him suffer even more the absence of love from souls? How might we fill with love the infinite longings of His soul? By enriching His soul — if I may be permitted the expression — with our kindness and our poor love.

Let us give Him everything, with kindness and tenderness and with the characteristic manner of a pure love. A love that does not seek itself, but which only desires to satiate His thirst for love. Let us try to unite ourselves so intimately with Jesus that His very Blood flows back and forth from His Heart to ours. For this is the reason that He lives in us.

Let us not be afraid that the weight of this love that we dream of giving Him might be too much for us. He desires that we share in His suffering. He is our very strength and He will always sustain us.

Prayer

O Heavenly Mother, teach us to love Him as you loved Him. We want to burn in the divine flame of His Love, to sacrifice ourselves without restrictions for Him. May no obstacle come between Jesus and ourselves. May there be only Jesus and only you, the Queen of Poverty and of Love! Amen.

21

HIS PURITY

"He is the image of the invisible God"
(Col 1:15).

One should approach the intimate sanctuary of Jesus — that Divine Heart — with the respectful silence and adoration of one who approaches the holy, removing from ourselves all that is human in order to penetrate into the depths of purity of that Heart which is all spotlessness and light.

The Heart of Jesus is a sanctuary of purity. It is the whiteness of the Eternal Light, the stainless mirror of Divine Majesty and the image of His Goodness (cf. 2 Cor 4:4).

Imagine the intimate depths of the Heart of Jesus. Ever sublime and perfect in Its purity. Ever divine, ever beautiful, with that beauty that is infinite and eternal: the Beauty of the God-Man! In Jesus, that which is divine appears with naturalness that is enchanting and breathtaking. No, Jesus does not exert Himself to produce sentiments that are divine and most pure, but makes an effort not to overwhelm our littleness with His Grandeur.

That which attracts us to the Heart of Jesus is the harmonious union of the divine with the human, which union has been divinized. Which resides in Him. If His purity were not human, or humanized, it would not be adaptable to us. If it were not divine, it could not satisfy us, nor could it make us like Him. But this Jesus, Who is Celestial Purity Himself, steals our hearts and causes us to fall in love with Him.

This Jesus is incomprehensible Fullness. He is an immense ocean of Light, of Grace and of Truth. He is Fullness because He encompasses every degree of holiness and His Heart possesses every degree of purity. His Heart is a bottomless treasure of all virtues to such a degree that each virtue is an abyss. These virtues form the ideal Model, to Whose likeness our own virtues should aspire. Jesus is Light, Love, and Purity! What human being could ever sound the depths of the divine virtues?

All of the fruits of Jesus' sacrifice are most pure. If we wish to enjoy those fruits of purity, we should participate in His sufferings and in His immolation. For suffering is also purity. This is how Jesus is! Let us live within the Heart of Jesus, because to live in Him is to live in heaven. That is, to live in light, in sacrifice and in purity. Let our conversation be in heaven.

Above all, let us live sharing in the intimate suffering of that Heart which is totally pure, but made sorrowful by redemptive suffering. Alleviating His pain by our sacrifices, living like this within Jesus' interior, and sacrificing ourselves for love of Him, we shall grow in purity.

Yes, Divine Heart! Yes, most loving Heart! Grant us this life of purity and sacrifice which we ask of You in the intimacy of our love!

Thank You, O Most Pure Heart of Jesus, thank You! For You broke open Your chest that we might count Your heartbeats of love! Grant that we might spread Your reign and cause souls to know Your interior martyrdoms, which have been so forgotten by the world, and Your Infinite purity.

Prayer

And you, O Mary, Immaculate Virgin! Jesus' fragrant lily! Obtain for us purity of body and soul, a heart filled with light and the soul of a child. May we never offend — even by thought — Jesus, Who is the Lily of the Valleys, the Brightness of Eternal Light, the Splendor of the Father. This Jesus Who is totally yours and ours as well. Amen.

22

HIS OBEDIENCE

*"Sacrifice and offering You did not desire,
but a body You prepared for Me; holocausts and sin
offerings You took no delight in. Then I said, 'As
is written of Me in the scroll, Behold, I come
to do Your will, O God'"* (Heb 10:6-7).

How could Jesus' obedience be anything but
perfect? *"He was obedient unto death... death on a
cross"* (Ph 2:8). He obeyed His eternal Father,
coming to the world to save it and He took on
flesh in the womb of a Virgin.

*"And it was thus that He humbled Himself, obe-
diently accepting even death, death on a cross. Because
of this, God highly exalted Him and bestowed on Him
the name above every other name, so that at Jesus'
Name every knee must bend in the heavens, on the
earth and under the earth, and every tongue proclaim
to the glory of God the Father: Jesus Christ is Lord"*
(Ph 2:8-11).

After being in the temple at the age of

twelve among the doctors of the law — who were amazed by the utmost wisdom of His questions and of His answers — He returned to Nazareth, where He remained until He was thirty years old, always obeying. Mary will also cause Him to hasten the hour of His miracles.

In all of His preaching and in the miracles that He performed, Jesus used His divine power and referred everything to the Father. He taught His doctrine and attributed it to His heavenly Father.

In the Garden of Olives, at the peak of the martyrdom of His Heart, with the most profound submission, He says, *"Father, not My will but Yours be done"* (Mt 26:39). *"Let not My will but Yours be done"* (Lk 22:41). He even repeated these same words, says St. Mark (14:39). From that moment on, He was no longer going to obey His eternal Father's, Mary's or St. Joseph's sweet orders, but would obey His merciless executioners, because His Father wanted it that way. An obedience that would cost Him His honor, torments, His blood and life itself! O, Jesus, You are that Man! May You be blessed!

He obeyed Pilate, who ordered Him to be scourged and judged and who sentenced Him to the most infamous death, that of the cross. He obeyed His executioners, who ordered Him to disrobe and to dress. They ordered Him to present His hands that they might be bound, and to bow His head in order to have it crowned with thorns. To bear the heavy cross, to get up after being beaten when He fell, to continue on to reach the place of torments, to lay Himself out upon the cross and allow Himself to be nailed to it. In obeying, Jesus made no distinction of persons, but rather was born, lived and died, obeying in order to manifest His love for the Father and by this means to save us.

Jesus, You know that we love You and that we wish to imitate Your virtues. Today, grant us the virtue of obedience, that we might submit our judgment and our will to God's. Grant us that forgetfulness of self that will separate us from ourselves and which will unite us more to You forever.

Prayer

O Holy Virgin, obtain for me the grace of never wasting the least opportunity to obey, because this is the indisputable road to holiness, to maintain interior peace, to please Jesus and to attain heaven. Amen.

23

HIS HUMILITY

*"Then He poured water into a basin and began
to wash the disciples' feet and dry them
with the towel around His waist"*
(Jn 13:5).

To look at Jesus is to see humility. *"Learn from
Me,"* He said during His passage through this
world, "not to be able to work miracles or to attain outstanding accomplishments, but *'to become
meek and humble of heart'"* (cf. Mt 11:29).

He suffered regarding His dignity, His
doctrine, His reputation, and His disciples. He
suffered in both His body and His soul in order
to teach us to decrease.

How humble Jesus was when He made
us aware of His abandonment by His heavenly
Father!

Who obliged Him to reveal to us this intimate secret of His soul, except His humility?

This is Jesus! That is why whoever loves needs to be humble. There is nothing in this world so sweet as to humble oneself for Jesus' sake.

Jesus was silent whenever He was accused. How often, despite the fact that He could have easily confounded His enemies, did Jesus prefer to be despised and humiliated! In order to cure our pride, Jesus endured insults and disgrace in silence.

O most humble Jesus, grant that we may recognize our own failings! More often than not, human praise is fickle, applause is hypocritical and honors are two-faced lies. But we believe them because they make us feel that we are something that we really are not. We allow pride to enter in and we distance ourselves from the truth.

How does one love God in a humble way? I am going to tell you:

"Love Me for Who I am, without self-seeking, without thinking about what you are going to get out of it. Love Me only because I am worthy of all love in heaven and on earth. Love Me without ever losing trust in My goodness, My merits, or My great mercy, whatever the circumstances may be. Finally, give yourself to others. Forget about yourself with a generous self-renunciation — unobtrusively — devoid of all self-interest and with the sole objective of giving Me glory.

"May your soul harbor no self-centered-ness, but let it communicate its fire, even if it were in a hidden way, on behalf of others. This will be the positive proof that your love for Me is a humble love."

Prayer

O sweet Virgin, come to our aid and let nothing separate us from the love of Jesus. Teach us to be faithful to the inspirations of grace and free us from our enemies, who wish us to fall into sin.

Grant us the courage and strength to resist our passions and give us a heart like yours. For we want to love Jesus as you loved Him: with that very profound humility of the "handmaid of the Lord." Amen.

24

HIS SENSITIVITY

"And whoever gives only a cup of cold water to one of these little ones to drink because he is a disciple — amen, I say to you, he will surely not lose his reward" (Mt 10:42).

Goodness is the most perfect beauty. Jesus offers an eternal reward for even a glass of water — for the least service. He never offends us and He always treats us with unrivaled finesse.

Jesus never lost His interior peace and He was always the same. He was easy to approach, sensitive to others, modest, humble, patient and loving. One did not have to make an appointment in order to speak with Him, because He was always willing to listen to each person who approached Him. That is how it was then, how it is now and how it always will be.

That is how Jesus is: all gentleness, goodness, finesse and mercy. That is love! A love that forgets everything. That consumes our failings in the Divine Flame of His Heart — Whose greatest happiness is to forgive, forget, embrace and save.

What joy it is to have Someone Who loves us like this! Who forgives us like this! Who forgets our ingratitude! Who has pity on our shortcomings! Jesus is so sensitive!

Let us live in the warmth of Jesus, resting in His love. Whether in sickness or in health, in life or in death, at peace or at war. Are not all these things really accidental and secondary compared to what is essential, namely, to love Jesus and to be loved by Him? Let us not lose our peace in any of the trials of life! Rather, let us live with the tranquility of one who possesses a treasure that nothing and nobody can take away from us. Let us live with the serenity of one who realizes to Whom he has entrusted himself or herself, secure in a love that is steadfast, tender, ardent and sensitive like Jesus' love is.

Let us meditate on the tenderness of His love and let us compare His immense charity with our own defects and failings. We should ask ourselves, "Have my faults and failings brought tears to the eyes of others and have they scandalized others?" We never offend the heart of another without also offending Jesus' Heart.

Today, let us offer Jesus the effort to always treat those around us with gentleness. May the sufferings which cause us to fall be not as if they had fallen on resounding bronze that leaves an echo, but as if they had fallen upon cotton or upon oil, allowing only a glimpse of the gentleness in which these blows are lost.

Our hearts should be like a calm sea in which resentments, betrayals, bitterness and all hues of self-love might be drowned, thinking only about Jesus' sensitivity, which always returned good for evil and which disguised and covered over others' failings, forgave offenses and forgot insults. He always paid back evil with goodness and love, pretending not to see our failings, forgiving our offenses, and forgetting how we have hurt Him.

Prayer

Jesus, I have been wounded many times, but I offer everything to You. Receive my sufferings on behalf of those who nail them into my heart. For, like You, I do not want to hurt others. Perhaps it will not be long until we see each other. I ask You to hasten Your possession of my soul, so that I may begin to live even here on earth with my heart in heaven, in the light, in Mary, in You, with the Father and with the Holy Spirit.

Mary, my Mother, I give myself to you without reserve, so that you might hide me within the Heart of your Divine Son. I give myself to you so that you might offer my immense gratitude for all His loving kindnesses with every breath I breathe, with every beat of my heart, with each palpitation of my soul. Amen.

25
HIS REPOSE

"He said to him the third time, 'Simon, son of John, do you love Me?' Peter was distressed that He had said to him a third time, 'Do you love Me?' and he said to Him, 'Lord, You know everything; You know that I love You'" (Jn 21:17).

The only thing that Jesus needs in order to rest is LOVE — a steadfast love, a humble love, a silent and holy love!

Love and humility! When we call to Him to come and rest in our hearts, Jesus wants to find there a very intense, very deep and very exquisite humility, because such humility does not close the doors to the soul, but instead opens them wide. Nor can Jesus find rest anywhere except in a gentle humility that adapts itself to His every longing.

When we want to rest we seek expansiveness and greatness. But Jesus looks for littleness, because He knows well that there is nothing greater on earth than that which is insignificant in the eyes of the world. His crib was small. His boat was small. His cross was small and narrow. Tabernacles are small, as are the Sacred Hosts and the souls that He chooses for His delight and repose.

How good Jesus is! How He delights in resting among the sons and daughters of man in spite of possessing heaven itself and the pure and loving bosom of His Beloved Father!

Jesus rests in the souls that know how to understand Him. "*I have called you friends, since I have made known to you all that I heard from My Father*" (Jn 15:15). But to His intimate friends He discloses His secrets with greater clarity and greater depth. As with His three chosen apostles, Peter, James and John, to whom He revealed the secret of His glory on Mount Tabor. They also saw the secret of His divine power in the home of Jairus and the secret of His suffering in Gethsemane.

But Jesus did not rest in any other soul as He did in Mary's, because her virginal and maternal heart reminded Him of the most loving bosom of the Father, which is Jesus' pre-eminent, Eternal, and Blessed Repose.

Souls of Light are simple souls, because it

is written, *"with the upright is His friendship"* (Pr 3:32). There is an intimate accord between God and simple persons, between Divine Wisdom and simplicity. Souls of Light are humble souls and it is God *"Who hides these things from the wise and intelligent, but reveals them to little ones"* (Lk 10:21). Jesus searches out these souls to be His repose.

If we are not pure, we want to be pure. If we are darkness, we want to be light. We want Him Who contains all virtues and then we shall form with that which is His a soft resting place in our soul.

The Eucharist and the Cross are immortal monuments that assure us that God's love is totally satisfying and eternal. Not even our sinful misery, nor our ingratitude, can lessen the love that Jesus has for us. This incomprehensible Love is not founded on the basis of our fleeting and fluctuating weaknesses, but upon the Immutable and Eternal Foundation of God's Goodness.

This is Jesus, Who seeks our hearts as a place of repose. Will we deny His request? Jesus, give us humility, purity and a love for You more than for anything else on earth.

Prayer

"Come, My beloved, to the manger that love changes into a throne; come to your Living Cross and rest peacefully in an ardent and firm love!"

Most Holy Virgin! We, too, want to be yours, only yours, always yours! We want to form a resting-place for Him in this life, so that we can rest in Him for all eternity. Amen.

26

HIS ABANDONMENT

"He kept saying, 'Abba, Father, You have the power to do all things. Take this cup away from Me. But let it be as You would have, not as I" (Mk 14:36).

Coming into this world, He said, *"Behold, I have come to do Your will"* (Heb 10:7). All of the thirty-three years of His lifetime on earth were spent in the faithful execution of the wishes of His Father, with a loving abandonment to that Divine Will. Even His sacrifice and His death were a total fulfillment of this Will, since as the Apostle teaches, *"By this [will] we have been sanctified through the offering of the body of Jesus Christ once for all"* (Heb 10:10).

At times, the Will of the Father was in contrast to Jesus' human will — as in Gethsemane. The bloody sweat barely expressed the intimate agony of Jesus' will. Nevertheless, in the middle of that cruel battle — from His lips and from the depths of His soul, as a cry of loving abandonment to His heavenly Father — burst forth the words, *"Not My will, but Yours be done!"* (Lk 22:42).

Not only did Jesus fulfill the will of the Father in its totality, but He always fulfilled it. There was never a single act of Jesus, nor a single instant of His life, in which Jesus sought His own will. In a real sense, He was never the master of His life or His actions, because His loving abandonment always voluntarily bound Him to the will of the Father.

What is the significance of Christ crucified? With regard to His Father, the very heart of the crucifixion lies in Jesus' abandonment to the Father's will, placing Himself unconditionally into His hands. From the Father toward Jesus, leaving Him in the cruelest of abandonments. But that abandonment — that crucifixion of the Father in Jesus — was the greatest act of love. It was a loving condescension to Jesus' longing to suffer in order to honor Him and to save souls.

Jesus bore all of our sins in order to expiate them. He wanted to experience that which was most difficult for His Heart — abandonment by God — in order to gain fortitude for us. And what did Jesus say in the midst of the infinite sea of His bitter abandonment? He exclaimed, full of resignation, *"Father, into Your hands I commend My spirit"* (Lk 23:46). This is an heroic attitude. It is confidence and sublime abandonment. The ultimate that love can offer.

Abandonment is the supreme expression of love, this giving of oneself without reserve to the Divine Will, which is the total gift of our very selves. This heroic attitude formed from inexpressible trust in God's Love, from perfect self-renunciation and from loving generosity, is the pinnacle of love.

That Divine Will shall also be our joy and our martyrdom. United to Jesus, what do sacrifices matter when love is consoled when it suffers? Each immolation, each cross, each sacrifice is the perfect fulfillment of the Father's will. That will is a joy and martyrdom — a Calvary and a heaven — because it encompasses all suffering and produces all joys. Oh, my abandoned Jesus, grant me Your love in abandonment, in loneliness and even in death itself!

Prayer

Lord, today grant that I no longer seek my personal satisfaction. Neither in that which is great, nor in that which is small. Neither in that which is divine, nor in that which is human. But help me to cast myself generously into personal sacrifice — into abandonment itself — if that should be Your will.

May I smilingly and full of joy "abandon myself up to the God Who abandons me." Solely out of love for Him. Solely for pure love of Him! O Mary — just Him! Just His love and His suffering! Because it is in suffering and in doing His will that saints are formed. Amen.

27

HIS PEACE

"It is He Who is our peace"
(Eph 2:14).

Jesus is peace. *"He is our peace,"* says St. Paul, for it is through Him that Infinite Peace became visible to our eyes and Infinite Peace became accessible to our longing. To give peace is to give Jesus. To possess peace is to possess Him. When a soul possesses Him, when He lives in the soul and the soul penetrates into His Heart — into His Intimacy — it finds its rest and it finds peace.

One possesses Jesus when all of the desires of the soul are focused on Him. When all of one's efforts for His glory have only Him as their object. When He is the only light of the soul and the only desire of the heart.

When all of the affections of the soul are blended into a single love — the love of Jesus

— there is peace. The heart that rests in this peace never loses its intimate tranquility. It sees Jesus in everything. It sees Him equally in contemplation as in activity. In times of suffering as in times of joy. In times of consolation as in those of desolation.

Peace is maintained only away from noise and away from the turmoil of our passions. Peace brings with it an interior silence that fills the soul with sweetness. The silence that comes from peace is not the silence of a desert, nor the silence of the tomb. It is a silence that comes from a Life that vibrates in the soul. It is the silence of a heart that has discovered Jesus and which loses itself contemplating Him — because He is our peace.

Peace is not something negative: a *lack* of conflict. It is rather something positive: a glimpse of heaven, a beam of tranquility and a ray of God's own happiness. The calm that comes from peace is not transitory, but is something that is permanent and immortal, like a day when the sun does not set.

Peace is the atmosphere that God Himself breathes, because it is the environment proper to love. That is why love demands solitude and silence — because it demands peace.

The person who is at peace is like a lake that is perfectly serene. A lake in which God is reflected. In which Jesus — the God-Man — is imaged.

To achieve that peace — that serenity — one needs a profound humility, a great purity of heart, a tranquil conscience and a trusting love, having no will outside of Jesus' will, nor any longing than that of pleasing Him in all things.

But even in suffering one receives love and peace of soul, for every pain is a caress from Jesus. One receives life because Jesus is Life. Suffering which we willingly accept brings us peace. It makes us like Him.

Prayer

Dear Jesus, I know that intimacy with You brings us to the fullness of peace and love and that if I enter thus into Your Heart, You shall freely enter into my heart. I need You to fulfill my mission, to carry my cross, and to keep myself in peace throughout the trials and difficulties of my life. I need You as my divine Cyrenian.

O Mary, more than any other creature you have known Jesus as He really is, the Prince of Peace. Help me that I might have no other desire than to sacrifice myself on behalf of others just to please Jesus, practicing many virtues in union with you, just to gratify Him. Amen.

28

HIS INTERNAL CROSS

*"My soul is filled with sorrow even to the
point of death"* (Mk 14:34).

If Jesus was all love, He was also all suffering. He
longed *"to be baptized with a baptism of blood"* (cf.
Lk 12:50). His external cross was as a relief, or
rest, compared to the interior suffering of His
Heart that crucified Him. From the moment of
His Incarnation, this inner cross oppressed Him
and throughout His life, the thorns of human
ingratitude pierced Him.

Jesus kept those sufferings hidden and
veiled. He smiled, worked and preached, but
He hid His interior suffering (which Mary sur-
mised), which He offered as the purest incense
to His Father in all the instances of His life.
The martyrdoms that tortured Him interiorly
are neither taken into account nor are they appreciated.

That little cross, which we contemplate

driven into the upper portion of Jesus' Heart, represents to us the most exquisite pain and a pain without relief. It is only in His prayer in the Garden of Gethsemane that He allows us a vague idea of the torture which, during His entire life, tore His innocent Heart to shreds.

Water and blood gushed forth from this Inner Sanctuary of Love to purify and save me. Jesus was willing to be left without blood, but not without me. He let His veins be drained for love of me. He opened the Fountain of Life so that my lips might drink and my soul might inebriate itself with purity and sanctity with this Wine that brings forth virgins.

Have I at least been grateful for these internal sufferings? Do I love them? Do I honor them? Do I meditate upon them? Do I make them known? Do I ask for them and do I embrace them in order to console Jesus?

If all the graces which we receive were solely the fruit of love, there would be motive enough to die of gratitude that we might make all the sacrifices in order to respond to that fervent love. But if they are also the fruit of sufferings — if to come forth from the Heart of Jesus, they tore it apart and they caused Him to shed blood — then where is there sufficient gratitude to appreciate them and adequate love to respond to them?

In this internal cross we find our salvation. This wound is the door to heaven, the manifestation of that longing with which the Heart of Jesus wanted to redeem us. From this sea of infinite Love, Eternal Happiness overflows in torrential streams.

Prayer

Although we do not deserve it, we open our arms and our whole soul with holy enthusiasm so that this Heart of Love can empty out its bitter sufferings into them, because we experience our greatest happiness when consoling Him.

At your side and with your help, Mary, what can we fear? I know that you are ever at the foot of Calvary. This being the case, let all the crucifixions come, because in the shadow of our blessed Mother nothing will be too hard for us, for we can do all things in Him Who comforts us. Amen.

29

HIS SACRIFICE

"No one takes away My life;
I freely give it up" (cf. Jn 10:18).

Jesus is the most perfect work of the Holy Spirit on earth. In Jesus, the most perfect work is His sacrifice. In His sacrifice, the most perfect work is immolation of His Heart.

"Then I said, 'I have come to do Your will, O God'" (Heb 10:7). The most Loving Will of the Father was that Jesus should sacrifice Himself for mankind in order to open the gates of heaven through His suffering.

When the hour assigned by His Father had arrived, He tore Himself away from Mary, His mother, whom He loved dearly, with the full knowledge that He was thrusting Himself into every kind of suffering and sacrifice, of hatreds and of persecutions, even to dying slandered on a scaffold for criminals, because that was the will of His beloved Father. Nor did He falter in the face of it. He heroically embraced every kind of suffering and martyrdom. He was not ignorant of the fact that His apostolate would have all its power and fruitfulness when the voice of His Blood would make itself heard throughout the universe from the cross.

For three hours, Jesus suffered unspeakable torments. His feet, that had tired themselves out seeking His wayward sheep, were nailed to the cross. As were His hands, which He had always used to do good for others. He besought His Father to forgive us (cf. Lk 23:34). It was there that He promised Paradise to the good thief (Lk 23:43). There that He suffered the cruelest torment, seeing Mary's sorrow. There that He gave her to us as mother and we were born within the heart of the sorrowing Virgin (cf. Jn 19:27).

It was there that Jesus cried out to heaven with the suffering of sufferings. When He felt, in the depths of His Being, abandonment by His beloved Father.

He was thirsty, but more than His physical thirst was His thirst for purity, for love, for virtues and for sacrifices that would glorify His beloved Father. When they gave Him vinegar to drink, He cried out, *"Now all is accomplished"* (Jn 19:30).

Resounding from the heights of the cross His vibrant, powerful voice, full of love and trust, cried out, *"Father, into Your hands I commend My spirit"* (Lk 23:46). Jesus died to give us life. He tells us in each crucifix that we see, "This is the way to love!"

Notwithstanding, Jesus fell three times on the way to Calvary and received blows and blasphemies from His executioners. How we should envy Simon of Cyrene who helped Jesus and had the good fortune to afford Him consolation! What do all of our sufferings matter if, with them, we are able to console Jesus?

Yes, Jesus, we love You and we want to show our gratitude for Your sacrifices by giving You cross for Cross, suffering for Suffering, love for Love! Our human nature shrinks from suffering, but the Holy Spirit provides grace and divine energy, giving us boldness and strength to conquer ourselves and to overcome our weakness.

Prayer

O Sorrowful Mary, you who knew how to share better than anyone else on earth in the sacrifices of Jesus, Your Son, obtain for us the grace to imitate Him and to sacrifice ourselves in union with Him, out of pure love. O how sweet death must be when one has lived upon the Cross! Amen.

30

HIS BLOOD

"He likewise took a cup, gave thanks and passed it to them: 'This is My blood, the blood of the covenant, to be poured out on behalf of many'"
(Mk 14:23-24).

Jesus could have saved a thousand worlds with a short prayer. Instead, He willed to shed all of His Blood to redeem us. Blood constitutes the essence of sacrifice, for blood is the means of reconciliation with heaven. It is the sign of covenant, which under the Old Law was poured out at the foot of the altar as a sign of expiation.

"*Almost everything,*" says the Apostle, "*is purified with blood. Without the shedding of blood there is no remission of sins*" (cf. Heb 9:22). Jesus, You gave Your Blood out of pure love for us and shed even the very last drop of it to open the gates of heaven for us. This is Jesus. Jesus is like that.

Jesus told us, "*He who drinks My blood will*

have eternal life and I will raise him up on the last day. Whoever drinks of this blood will have eternal life" (Jn 6:54). Jesus shed His Blood to save us, so that we might not perish in eternal Death. So that for all eternity we might enjoy the fruits of His sacrifice and live a true life with Him, Who is Life itself.

Even after dying for us, Jesus wanted to demonstrate His love. He left the climax of His infinite Love and Mercy. He allowed a lance to open His side, leaving a wide wound through which His Heart poured out the last drop of His Blood which, mingled with water, would wash clean the whole world. That Divine Blood of the God-Man is present in the sacraments. It is the treasure of the Church and the salvation of the world.

O Jesus, may I never lose sight of You like this, pouring out Your Blood for love of me! I want to enter into the depths of love of Your Sacred Heart and never leave! You, Who shed all of Your Blood to save me and to obtain for me the grace of purity and a happy eternity, grant that I might ever live within You.

Prayer

O Sorrowful Mary, tear from me this heart of ice and give me a new one, O Mother, that will know how to be grateful for your favors. I am ashamed of my ingratitude, my sins, my lukewarmness and my lack of attention. I am not worthy to be called your child, Mother, but I know that even if it were to cost your life, they could never erase from your Heart the love, the tenderness and the mercy that you feel for your children. Amen.

31

HIS EUCHARIST

"I am the bread of life.
Whoever comes to Me will not hunger,
and whoever believes in Me will never thirst"
(Jn 6:35).

The Eucharist is the compendium of all of the marvels of God and the consummation of all the mysteries that He brings about in souls. The Eucharist perpetuates all of the mysteries of Jesus and makes them present to us who were not alive when He was on earth. Through the Eucharist we can transport ourselves to Bethlehem, being exhilarated with the sweetness of that unforgettable night. Through it we breathe the silent surroundings of Nazareth, we perceive the scenes of the Lake of Tiberias and we hear the words of eternal life. By means of that beloved Eucharist, we glimpse in heavenly moments the glory of Tabor. We taste something of the intimate bitterness of Gethsemane and we are present at the sorrowful tragedy of Calvary as it renews itself mystically upon the altar.

Let us live with Jesus in Holy Communion and He will live within us and will communicate to us all that He is. Let us cast far from us tepidity and indifference. Let us come to the altar with our soul on fire. With an insatiable longing to receive Jesus. Like the little child who casts himself upon his mother's breast, or like one with an insatiable thirst who comes to a crystalline spring of living water.

How grateful we should be to Jesus for His Eucharist!

All His gifts seemed minor to Him, so He made Himself the gift, giving us His Body, His Soul, His Blood and His Divinity!

How might we ever repay Him for that heavenly Food?

Why is it unusual that souls should reach the heights of consummation if they are fed on unity, if they are fed on Jesus, Who is the fruit of unity and its unquenchable Source? Jesus is Unity, because He is Purity. Because He is Light. Because He is Love. Because He is the Glory of the Father. What might He produce in souls but perfect Unity, especially when He is divinely disposed to realize that Unity in the Eucharist? Let us partake of this divine Food so that our soul might be consumed in Unity.

"Allow me to suffer," said St. Ignatius of Antioch, "I am the wheat of God. I want to be ground by the teeth of the beasts in order to become the Immaculate Bread of Christ." St. Bernard also said, "When our Savior gives Himself to me as food, He nourishes Himself; His joy consists in all the good that He finds within me." This is Jesus, Who has an insatiable hunger for us. Who knows that we are poor. Who comes to enrich us with that Bread, that whoever eats it will never hunger again.

Let us offer the Incarnate Word unceasingly to our Heavenly Father within our hearts. Let us unite ourselves to all His immolations on behalf of His beloved Church and in thanksgiving for that Gift of gifts — the Holy Eucharist. Let us make reparation to the most Holy Sacrament of the altar for the times we have forgotten Him. For the ingratitude and the sins of so many souls who, in the Blessed Sacrament, wound the loving Sacred Heart of Jesus in its most intimate recesses.

Prayer

Undoubtedly, it was primarily for you, Mary, that Jesus instituted the Sacrament of Love. If He was not willing to leave us orphans when He ascended into heaven, how could He abandon you in exile without living at your side? Without leaving you His Body, His Soul, His Heart and His Divinity during the years of your solitude on earth?

Obtain for us today from Jesus, that He might pour out, over those of us who love Him so much in the Eucharist, all the blessings that He sends to the world by means of the consecrated Hosts. Amen.

32

HIS PRIESTS

"I consecrate Myself for them,
that they also may be consecrated in truth"
(Jn 17:19).

What was it that Jesus loved with the greatest preferential love? His mother and His Church, the depository of His doctrine and His Heart, of His very self in the Eucharist. In the plan of salvation, the Church was the fulfillment of Jesus' mission on earth, because Jesus entrusted to her not only His teachings and His salvific and sanctifying power, but He Himself remained in it until the end of time.

After He had died and risen, Jesus sent His Holy Spirit that, by His Light, the apostles might understand all that He had taught them. *"It is better for you that I go. For if I do not go, the Advocate will not come to you"* (Jn 16:7). *"The Holy Spirit, that the Father will send in My name, will teach you everything and remind you of all that I told you"* (Jn 14:26).

Jesus built His Church upon Peter. He gave him the keys to the Kingdom of Heaven and He bestowed the power to bind and to loose upon him: *"Peter, do you love Me?... Feed My lambs.... Feed My sheep"* (Jn 21:15-17). From that moment on, Peter — and in him all of his successors — became the head of the Church, with the power to open for us the portals of grace and the gates of heaven.

The Holy Spirit communicates Himself to priests through their ordination, imprinting the priestly character — which is a participation in the Priesthood of Jesus — on their being. The foundation of the priesthood is the Holy Spirit. Its essence is an intimate union with Jesus. When forming a priest, the Holy Spirit unites him to the Supreme and only Priest, making of him another crucified Jesus.

What would we do if there were no priests in the world? Without priests, how would God's blessings be applied to us? What good would a house full of gold be to us, if we did not have someone who could open the door for us? The priest has the key to the heavenly treasures. He opens that door for us. He is the administrator of all its goods. If there were no priests, there would be no Eucharist. There would be no Reconciliation where Jesus forgives our short-comings and obtains graces for us with His immolation. Where He increases our glory and brings souls out of Purgatory.

What an obligation we the faithful have to sacrifice ourselves in union with Jesus for His priests in order to shore up their spiritual strength, since we owe them so much and we have cost them so much! How little gratefulness we show these souls who sacrifice themselves for us. Who offer up their lives, no longer belonging to themselves. Who give us Jesus!

One might define the priest as he who glorifies the Father through the sacrifice of Jesus under the influence of the Holy Spirit. This is Jesus the Eternal Priest; the only Priest Who has made of His priests a continuation of His very own Self on earth. They are "other Christs," who will bring us to Him.

Prayer

Mary, with what love you must have inflamed the hearts of the apostles so that they might spread the Church. So that they might joyfully shed their blood and give their lives to uphold Jesus' cause: the truth and the faith! You, who were the light of the apostles, the fire who caused them to burn, thirsting to communicate the doctrine they had received to souls. Help priests — that chosen portion whom Jesus loves so much — and unite them to yourself. Console them, fortify them and daily teach them — in ever greater depth — what Jesus is like and how He wishes them to be other Christs. Amen.

33

HIS DEEPEST DESIRES

"Remain in My love. You will remain in My love if you keep My commandments"
(Jn 15:9-10).

Oh Jesus, You are content with this. What else could satisfy Your thirst for love better than that we should remain in Your love, keeping Your commandments? Love is the essence of perfection and the source of peace. It is a tiny speck of heaven itself. It is love that gives us God and that causes us to surrender to Him. Love is everything, because *"God is love"* (1 Jn 4:16).

Speaking of love, there are not only moments when Jesus comes to the soul and moments when the soul goes toward God, but there are also those times when both simultaneously fling themselves, one toward the other, and they meet on the way. This is delightful, because the impact of these two loves coming together as one produces fire.

United to Him and remaining in His love, let Him send us whatever He wishes to send us. Let Him immolate us upon the cross that He desires, since we belong to Him and He is free to do as He wishes with what belongs to Him.

Let us strive, by our purity of heart, to become a clear mirror that continuously reproduces the portrait of Jesus within ourselves. That reflects His interior feelings faithfully, so that our soul might weep when He is sad, might rejoice when He is happy. Let us become like a harp that reproduces — without the least variation — the divine notes that vibrate within His Heart. What a joy it is to live with Jesus, to live of Jesus and to live in Jesus, loving Him and offering ourselves to Him without reserve. This is how we will remain in His love.

It is in suffering that one learns to love and to remain in Jesus crucified, in Jesus humiliated, in Jesus immolated. United to Him, nothing will be too much for us. In union with Him, our own sacrifices will have merit. By our remaining in Him, *the world will come to know that we are His disciples* (Jn 13:35), that we belong to Him.

O Jesus, if I were able to steal something from You, I would steal only love, so that I could love You more.

How often Jesus hides amid clouds of desolation and helplessness! How many times we do not find Him because He is hidden! But if Jesus lets us share something of His bitter suffering, how blessed we are! He is with us in the midst of tribulation.

In the desolations of life, in the storms and temptations in which our soul struggles in the dark night of the spirit, in the pain and agony that afflicts our heart — it is then that we are able to prove to Jesus that we do remain in His love, with humility and trust.

It is not possible to separate love and suffering in this life. It would be easier to separate fragrance from a flower than to separate those two modes of the same reality — love and suffering. How delightful it is to love Jesus and to live with Him and in Him. How delightful it is to do His will in the midst of suffering! In times of happiness and in times of intense suffering, always, always, we should remain in His love.

Prayer

O Mary, there was not a single moment of your precious life that you did not remain in Jesus' love! Most faithful Virgin! Without equal in your correspondence to the inspirations of the Holy Spirit! You were always faithful to the Eternal Father in your obedience. Faithful to Jesus in every circumstance of your life. Obtain for us the grace to remain always in the love of Jesus, that we may please Him and fulfill His desire in that which He asks of us today as the finishing touch of this series of meditations: *"Remain in My love"* (Jn 15:9). Amen.

34

HIS LOVE FOR MARY

*"When the fullness of time had come,
God sent His Son born of a woman, born under the
law, to rescue those under the burden of the law,
that they might receive adoption as sons
and daughters" (Gal 4:4-5).*

How Jesus must have loved His most Holy Mother! He was so loving, so tender and so grateful to her! It was to her, through the action of the Holy Spirit, that He owed His human life. To her that He owed His body that would be crucified, His blood that would redeem us and His Eucharist that would nourish us! What must have been His burning love for that Mother, so innocent, so pure and without any stain of sin?

Jesus, as we conclude these meditations about You and what You are really like, would You like to tell us Your thoughts and feelings at the side of Your sinless and most Holy Mother?

(Jesus speaks):

"I used to rejoice when I thought about her place in the mystery of the Incarnation. When I, as God, became man and the Holy Spirit infused into the Heart of Mary an ocean of love for her beloved Son, Who was, at one and the same time, her son and her God. Mary's love, from that blessed moment, was the sweetest and most special of all loves, because it was a true reflection of the love of My heavenly Father.

"For thirty years I witnessed, in our hidden life in Nazareth, the heroic virtue of My mother. Her care and solicitude for My every want, giving up sleep and totally sacrificing herself to help and please Me. Mary was able to read My soul like an open book. She saw concerns that used to absorb my thinking and the suffering that tortured Me. She used to see Me pray to the Father and offer Myself over and over to be sacrificed in order to save fallen mankind.

"It was consoling for Me to speak to her about the Holy Eucharist, about My apostolate, about you who are reading this and listening to Me; to tell her about My desire to suffer and die with a baptism of blood. About My Church in the future, which would cost Me My life on the cross. Her own martyrdom, so heroic and innocent, pained Me deeply.

"The Holy Spirit filled her with graces so that she could love more intensely and could suffer without measure for Me, Who was beginning to live in the *souls of men and women. The Holy Spirit enabled her to conceive all of her future children in love and in sorrow. These children who, participating in My life through grace, would imitate her here on earth until the end of time.*

"The final outpouring of the Holy Spirit on the soul of My beloved mother was so intense and ardent, so impetuous and divine, that Mary, although she had previously experienced God's love, was unable to withstand it. She died in love, because of her love and so actually died of Love Itself."

Prayer

My Mother! Is not this the word that expresses all of your dignity, all of your graces, your special gifts, and your mission in heaven and on earth? Mother of God! Mother of mankind! Mother — the word and the name that speaks of your ineffable and maternal love for Jesus and us — for Jesus in His human body and in His Mystical Body. Mary, our heavenly Mother, look upon us with compassion, and we beg you never to leave us. Amen.

CONCEPCIÓN CABRERA DE ARMIDA

She was a Mexican woman, wife,
mother and lay apostle.

Half a million copies of her books were
distributed — without her name being used
— in Spain and Latin America during her
lifetime. These books continue to set hearts
on fire with the love of Jesus and with a
burning desire to collaborate in the salvation
of men and women throughout the world.

This servant of God was born
in San Luis Potosí on December 8, 1862, and
died in México City on March 3, 1937.
The cause for her beatification is moving
forward. She was declared Venerable
by Pope John Paul II on December 20, 1999.